W9-BYG-525

Also by Louis Jenkins

Sea Smoke

The Winter Road

Just Above Water

Nice Fish

All Tangled Up with the Living

An Almost Human Gesture

NORTH OF THE CITIES

NORTH OF THE CITIES

50 Prose Poems and a conversation with Garrison Keillor

LOUIS JENKINS

Will o' the Wisp Books
Duluth, Minnesota

Published by Will o' the Wisp Books 2007
Printed in Canada
Second Printing 2008

Cover painting by Margot McLean, *10 Crows*, 2001, mixed media, 22 x 22 in.
Cover design by Amy Burkett

ISBN 13 978-0-9793128-0-9
ISBN 0-9793128-0-9

Some of the poems in this book originally appeared in the following publications: *Bare Root Review, Magma, Paterson Literary Review, The Rake, Redactions, Willow Springs*

Special Thanks to Amy Burkett, Robert Olen Butler, Anne-Marie Fyfe, James Hillman, Ann Jenkins, Garrison Keillor, Margot McLean, Chris Monroe

Louis Jenkins is a fiscal Year 2007 recipient of a Career Development grant from the Arrowhead Regional Arts Council (www.ARACouncil.org) which is made possible through an appropriation from The McKnight Foundation.

Will o' the Wisp Books
101 Clover Street
Duluth, Minnesota
55812-1103
www.willothewispbooks.com

For Lars and Amy

CONTENTS

I.

II.

III.

I

LEGEND

As you grow older you begin to enter the world of myth, you become less a fact and more a legend. The word becomes flesh and then gradually becomes word once more. You exist mainly as the stories people tell about you, full of inconsistencies, inaccuracies and downright lies. Anything else, what's really happening, isn't very interesting. But then, the stories most people tell aren't that good either. You can see this. The lives of the people you know become harder and harder to believe.

WINTER DAY

It is one of those dark winter days with a heavy snow falling. I start to move a chair from its place in the corner and suddenly realize someone had been sitting there in the shadows all along. "Oh! I'm sorry!" "Oh, no problem," he says, as he jumps up. I try replacing the chair, but it's no use. He stands at the window, hands folded behind his back, watching the snow fall in the yard. "Would you like some tea?" "No, no, I'm fine." I feel as though I should know this person; that he is here out of some courtesy to me. "This snow is really coming down," he says. "Yes," I say. "I should be going before the roads get too bad." He stands at the window and does not move. "Yes," I say.

THE AFTERLIFE

Older people are exiting this life as if it were a movie...
"I didn't get it," they are saying.
He says, "It didn't seem to have any plot."
"No." she says, "it seemed like things just kept coming at me. Most of the time I was confused... and there was way too much sex and violence."
"Violence anyway," he says.
"It was not much for character development either; most of the time people were either shouting or mumbling. Then just when someone started to make sense and I got interested, they died. Then a whole lot of new characters came along and I couldn't tell who was who."
"The whole thing lacked subtlety."
"Some of the scenery was nice."
"Yes."
They walk on in silence for a while. It is a summer night and they walk slowly, stopping now and then, as if they had no particular place to go. They walk past a streetlamp where some insects are hurling themselves at the light, and then on down the block, fading into the darkness.
She says, "I was never happy with the way I looked."
"The lighting was bad and I was no good at dialogue," he says.
"I would have liked to have been a little taller," she says.

FIGURE STUDIES

What do you do when you want to write but can't think of a thing, not a word? I think composers have it better, they can at least play the scale if they can't think of a tune: do re mi fa.... A painter has all that color, and if you ran out of ideas, you could do yet another self-portrait, or get a model and do figure studies. Maybe that's what I need, a model, an attractive young woman. I'd say, "Lie down on that couch, my dear, open your dressing gown just a bit more. Like that, yes," ...and I would write in my notebook, "Your lips are like petals.... Your teeth are like the stars...."

BIG BROWN PILLS

I believe in the big brown pills: they lower cholesterol and improve digestion. They help prevent cancer and build brain cells. Plus, they just make you feel better overall. I believe in coffee and beet greens and fish oil, of course, and red wine, in moderation, and cinnamon. Green tea is good and black tea and ginseng. I eat my broccoli. Nuts are very good, and dark chocolate—has to be dark, not milk chocolate. Tomatoes. But I think the big brown pills really help. I used to believe in the little yellow pills, but now I believe in the big brown pills. I believe that they are much more effective. I still take the little yellow ones, but I really believe in the big brown ones.

A NEW POEM

I am driving again, the back roads of northern Minnesota, on my way from A to B, through the spruce and tamarack. To amuse myself I compose a poem. It is the same poem I wrote yesterday, the same poem I wrote last week, the same poem I always write, but it helps to pass the time. It's September and everything has gone to seed, the maple leaves are beginning to turn and the warblers are on their way south. The tansy and goldenrod in the ditches are covered with dust. Already my hair has turned gray. The dark comes much earlier now. Soon winter will come. I sigh and wonder, where has the time gone?

LAW OF THE JUNGLE

We die of silliness, finally. Remember all those nights of wine, the heated discussion, the smoky room, the music? Those questions you pondered then have no relevance "Why do we live?" you asked. More to the point now is, "Where do I live?" First you forget to zip, then as time goes by you forget to unzip. There is a banana peel around every corner. Remember all those powerful, intense things you said back then, how the girls found you powerful and intense? You couldn't say those things with a straight face now, and anyway, those girls weren't really listening. The old lion, with patchy mane and sagging belly stands up to guard his territory. He gives a pathetic roar and the hyenas die laughing.

WHEN IT GETS COLD

When it gets cold around here we like to throw hot water into the air and watch it become instant ice mist that drifts away, never hitting the ground. Sometimes we drive nails with a frozen banana. Sometimes we just watch the numbers on the gas and the electric meters go spinning by. There's just no end to the fun.

But things get weird when it gets very cold. Things you never imagined come to life. There's an insect that appears, some kind of fly. Trees and houses make strange noises, and there are spooky, misty shapes moving around in the woods. Once when it was twenty-five below I found bare human footprints in snow that had fallen just a few hours before.

Everyone gets a little crazy when it's very cold for several weeks. Some people go in for compulsive house cleaning, others read, read everything: milk cartons, shipping labels.... We eat too much. We sleep a lot too. Once, during a cold spell, I slept for three days and when I woke I drank a gallon and a half of coffee.

AMBITION

One of the good things about getting older is that no one asks anymore "What are you going to be when you grow up?" Or later on, "What do you do?" Questions for which I never had a good answer. Nowadays everyone assumes I'm retired, and that I have no ambition whatsoever. It isn't true. It is true that it's too late for me to become an Olympic champion swimmer or a lumberjack, but my ambitions are on higher things. I want to be a cloud. I'm taking some classes and have a really good instructor. I don't want to be a threatening storm cloud, just one of those sunny summer clouds. Not that I won't have a dark side, of course. I'd like to be one of those big fat cumulus clouds that pass silently overhead on a beautiful day. A day so fine, in fact, that you might not even notice me, as I sailed over your town on my way somewhere else, but you'd feel good about it.

NONFICTION

I don't like it when someone else's fantasy world interferes with my own. That's why I don't read novels much anymore or watch television. I don't go for nonfiction either. Fiction and nonfiction aren't opposites. It isn't truth vs. lies. Nonfiction is simply not fiction— it's something else, I don't know what. Take the president, for example, from what I read in the newspapers, (which, as I am led to believe, are nonfiction,) can't be real. He has to be made up by some really bad writer. Unless I imagined all that stuff.

CLEAN UP

We invited some people over for drinks because they seemed nice and we thought it would be fun. They're about our age, a little younger maybe, and we have some things in common. They are coming this evening so now we have to clean the place up. What a drag. But we can't let them think that we are slobs, that we leave the morning oatmeal to dry hard in the pot, that the sink is full of yesterday's dirty dishes, that the kitchen table is piled high with books and magazines and coffee-stained papers, that the bed is unmade and the floor needs vacuuming. We can't let it appear that we are the kind of people who forget to change the car oil or mow the goddamn lawn; that we have completely lost our grip. We want them to know that we have not succumbed, that we can maintain order in the midst of all this chaos.

A PLACE OF YOUR OWN

It is so good to have a place of your own, a comfortable bed, a place where in the evening you can hide away from all the defeat of the day, a place where you know where things are, or at least you know in which pile a particular item might be found. But suppose one day the place gets ransacked while you are away. Maybe you're lucky, maybe it was only the three bears, but the place is a mess, your neat stack of L.L. Bean catalogs strewn all over. They've eaten everything; even that jar of pickled Brussels spouts way at the back of the fridge. Even after you get it all cleaned up it's not the same as it was. "You have to move on," a friend of mine says, "at our age we can just close the door and go away, take a trip to China or Hot Springs. Just think of it as practice for not being here at all."

EVOLUTION

I think it's okay not to like the idea of evolution. I can understand how one would not like to think of oneself as distantly related to a lemur, since most of us are none too fond of some of our more immediate relatives. But it seems to me that evolution is the least of our worries. For years I have accepted things as they are, or seem to be, without thinking much about them. Not now. Now, I have come to realize that I don't approve of gale-force winds or high water, or volcanoes or earthquakes. The idea of tectonic plates doesn't appeal to me. The idea that we are dependent on gravity to keep us on the ground makes me queasy—the idea that there is no up or down and we are merely sticking out from the planet. I don't at all like the idea of flight, except for birds. I don't even enjoy riding in automobiles. I believe, even though I do not practice it, that we should walk everywhere we go. But then there's the problem of standing, balance and all that. I'm not so sure that just two legs is a good idea.

WHERE WE LIVE

It's easy to get lost in the woods around here, to wander around in circles, not 50 feet away from the path and never see it. Beneath the canopy of trees not even your GPS will work. It leads to a lot of uncertainty. So if you come to visit I can't be very specific with my directions. I can only give you probabilities. We leave a lot of notes around as indicators: "Dentist Thur. 9:30," "Eggs," "Pick up Mom." It doesn't always work. "Honey, what's this blank Post-It note stuck to the bathroom mirror all about?" "Oh, nothing," she says.

PARSIMONIOUS

What a luxury, what a gift to have had a life, more or less, my own, to wander, la-de-da, beneath the quaking aspen with leaves like $100 gold pieces and the blue, blue sky. And what shall I do with such riches? Give them away. Give them parsimoniously to family and friends, to those I love and those who love me, and give them in great abundance to strangers: thieves, con artists, drunks, politicians; wastrels like myself.

II

SPIDER

An entrepreneurial spider has built her web between the bars of the railing at the scenic overlook in order to catch small insects blown in on the lake wind. If you can stick around she'll tell you all about the difficulties of owning a small business.

STARFISH

It seems like starfish don't do anything, but actually they move along at a rate of about 60 feet per hour. A starfish will eat anything that moves slower than it does, which excludes a great number of dishes from its diet. A starfish is all arms and appetite; it has no brain, yet in spite of this, time-lapse photography has shown that the starfish maintains an active social life. So in these regards the starfish is like many of the people you know.

EARL

In Sitka, because they are fond of them, people have named the seals. Every seal is named Earl because they are killed one after another by the orca, the killer whale; seal bodies tossed left and right into the air. "At least he didn't get Earl," someone says. And sure enough, after a time, that same friendly, bewhiskered face bobs to the surface. It's Earl again. Well, how else are you to live except by denial, by some palatable fiction, some little song to sing while the inevitable, the black and white blindsiding fact, comes hurtling toward you out of the deep?

SEAGULLS

There were no seagulls in the harbor, none at the marina. I saw none in the air. There were no seagulls at Canal Park, or McDonald's, or at Russ Kendall's smokehouse, or at the Kmart parking lot, or any of their favorite hangouts. It's winter and snow is falling, but I don't believe seagulls fly south. I've often seen them standing around on the ice all day, as if they were waiting for a big bus to come and take them to a casino. Where are all the seagulls? This is not a question I ever thought I'd ask myself. You get used to someone being around and if they go away you miss them. That's how life is. But seagulls are primarily a nuisance, and if you can't count on that, what can you count on?

LARGE DOG

A dog would be the thing, she thought, now that she lived alone, a big dog that looked rather scary and barked, a watchdog, but one that was actually gentle, a companion, a big, lovable fur ball. She adopted a dog from the pound, Walter, who was part German shepherd and part golden retriever. She got all his shots and had him neutered. She got a retractable leash for walks, morning and evening, after work. Walk time. Walter is happy, sniffing and pulling this way and that. She calls and pulls back. She has a big dog on a leash but she is going where he wants to go.

HORSE

It was probably a collection of human vices that led to the domestication of the horse: *envy* (I wish I could run that fast), *laziness* (If I rode on the back of the horse it would be much easier than walking), *greed* (just think how many rabbits I could kill), *vanity* (just think how good I'd look, all in black, on the back of that great white stallion). It took a brave soul to be the first one to ride a horse. He or she, no doubt, approached the horse slowly, whispering, "Nice horsey, here is a carrot for you. I'm going climb very gently and carefully onto your back and if you throw me off I'm going to hit you over your big stupid head with this big oak board." Having been a passenger on a horse once or twice, I understand the rush to invent the automobile. Nowadays the horse is ridden mostly for pleasure, if you can call it that. Personally, I prefer to watch horses: powerful bays and sorrels, pintos and roans running, muscles rippling, running across the plains, over the hills and far away.

BOWERBIRD

The satin bowerbird builds his bower carefully, a construction of twigs and grass, and carefully decorates it with display items, blue feathers, blue bottle caps, blue bits of paper and potsherds. His feathers are blue and he likes blue, and more to the point, the female bowerbird likes blue. During the mating season the bower is constantly rearranged and rebuilt. The bower isn't a nest, it's an elaborate construction designed to lure female bowerbirds. So it's like theoretical physics or poetry, hard work and essentially useless, except for the sex. And in most cases the female bowerbird doesn't even take a second look at what she considers to be a second-rate bower. She has an eye. She knows immediately a bower worthy of her close inspection. The bower builder is preening and doing his little song and dance. "You wouldn't *believe* how far I had to fly with that bottle cap in my beak." She likes the look of this bower, likes the way those twigs are arranged, just so. Likes the little touches of red plastic, here and there among the blue things. Yes, this is a bird that can build a better bower, should she ever need one. So perhaps she'll just step inside.

BAT

There's a bat circling in the early dark, between the pine tree, the spruce and the maple. He seems happy enough gobbling up perhaps hundreds of mosquitoes on each turn around. But maybe it's Dracula. You have to think about that. Maybe Dracula doesn't transform himself into bat; instead maybe the bat becomes Dracula. He has to go home soon, put on his little suit and tie and wander around the empty castle muttering to himself in a strange accent. And later, of course, there will be guests for dinner.

SQUIRREL

The squirrel makes a split-second decision and acts on it immediately— headlong across the street as fast as he can go. Sure, it's fraught with danger, sure there's a car coming, sure it's reckless and totally unnecessary, but the squirrel is committed. He will stay the course.

FISH/FISHERMAN

The fish are either off or on. Day after day there are no fish, only wind and waves, and seagulls waiting patiently. Then the fish are on. They come from nowhere, suddenly alive and turning and flashing in unison, uncles, cousins, daughters. All fish are one fish but their combined intelligence cannot outwit a gill net. Then the fish are off and lie in the bottom of the boat with x's for eyes.

After I've cleaned the fish and sold most of the day's catch, I bring a few home for supper. I always put one fish out on the stump beside the shed. In the morning the fish is gone. I don't know what takes it, if it's a weasel or a raccoon or a bear or a crow. I don't watch, or try to track whatever it is. I put the fish out in the evening, and in the morning it's gone.

ART

I decided that it would be nice to be someone else for a change. I call myself Art. Being someone else is kind of like having a guest, so my job is to make Art feel welcome and happy. What would Art like? Art would like coffee, I think, so off I go. When I meet someone I say "How do you do? Name's Art." If I meet someone I know already they say, "Your name is Lou, not Art, you have always been Lou." "Oh, all right then, call me Lou." (Art is a very easy-going guy) I just don't see why people have to be so inflexible, so unequivocal, so... definite. Meanwhile, I have learned that Art likes baseball, so I've got a ticket to this afternoon's Twins game.

CHAMELEON

I used to have a girlfriend named Jane Kieffer, from San Diego. She was beautiful and she was a chameleon. She could appear to be a small and waif-like blond or a tall redhead, to suit her whim, or mine. She would change her style, her look, her demeanor, almost instantly it seemed. She could be sophisticated or earthy, depending my momentary needs, and the surroundings. She was fantastic, great at parties and when we were alone. She always knew just the right moves. The trouble was I didn't know what I wanted. It seemed, as a couple, we lacked any focus, any stability. She began to anticipate my moods and change in advance. It drove me crazy. "Who are you, why are you like this?" I asked. She said she was born in the sea and that she had no soul. "What about me?" "You have none either," she said. I was often angry and she would cry, or worse, sit impassively and say nothing, blending into the background. One day I pulled on my pants and said, "That's it. I'm leaving." I never saw her again—or else we got married and raised a family. I'm not sure.

DON'T GET AROUND
MUCH ANYMORE

"Barbara, it is so good to see you! How are you getting along since your divorce?" "Why, Ellen, my divorce was twenty years ago! I'm fine."
"No! Twenty years, it can't have been that long?"
"Yes."
"How are your children?"
"They're both doing well, Jeff lives in Seattle and works for Microsoft. He and his wife have two boys, Evan and Lyle. Lyle is still in high school and Evan is in his second year at MIT studying engineering. Mara lives in Chicago and works for an ad agency. She's doing well, she and her partner are remodeling an old farmhouse near Oshkosh, so she's very busy, all that driving back and forth."
"And how about yourself, Barbara?"
"Oh, I'm very busy as well, work at the church, I work with the AAUW and I still play golf when I can."
"That's so good Barb! I think it's important to stay involved after a divorce. It's been so good to see you and remember, Barb, these things just take time."

MARRIAGE

He said, "People say marriage is like a three-legged race, but in our case she and I are tied together facing in the opposite directions on the stairs— she heading toward the main floor with the carpets and the furniture and such, and me heading to the basement with the furnace and the laundry tubs. It's okay, we get along, going nowhere, but it's damned difficult for the children or anyone else to get by us, whichever way they are headed."

THE COMMON COLD

It was something you said, no doubt, while half asleep.
Some meaningless rant that took on a life of its own.
That someone breathed in, misunderstood, and
breathed out. That mutated like all gossip, that went
away and was gone for years, prodigal son working at
the pizza parlor, accumulating a list of grudges, never
getting the respect he thought was his due, and every
day planning his return.

THE RAVEN

"I'm really a princess," the raven said from its perch on a pine branch. "Really?" I said, acting as though I was not at all surprised to be conversing with a raven.

"My evil stepmother put a curse on me. A spell that can only be broken by a prince. I can see from here that you are no prince. Do you happen to be a wizard?

"No, I'm sorry."

"I just thought, since you have this little shack in the woods, you might be a wizard. I had a wizard once, not a very good wizard I'm afraid. He was the one told me that I'd need a prince. A prince who loved me and would perform all kinds of difficult and time-consuming tasks. These tasks involved giants, gloomy forests, castles, high mountains, that sort of thing. I must have gone through half-a-dozen princes and none of them were up to it. Most of them turned out to be toads. They all married commoners and live really dull-normal lives now. Then one day I found my man. He was handsome, he was crazy about me, and he would do anything for me, slay dragons, sail the widest seas... But when he had finished all the tasks... nothing. Nothing changed! I was still a raven. There were accusations, recriminations. The prince said I'd tricked him, that I wasn't really a princess. I said he'd never even *seen* a dragon let alone slain one. We had a bitter parting. I flew back to find the wizard but he'd gone out of business. Moved. No forwarding address. I searched for a year, even hired a private investigator, but never found him. I don't suppose he could have helped me anyway. He was a lousy wizard. I've been a raven so long now that I've almost gotten used to it.... Are you sure you aren't a wizard?"

"I'm sure. Just a guy who has a shack in the woods."

"You don't have a cloak that makes you invisible?"

"No."

"No seven league boots?"

"No."

"How about a dead rabbit then?"

IF IT WAS A SNAKE

You've lost something, your car keys, or your watch and you have searched for what seems like hours. But then suddenly it appears, right there on the table, not two feet away. "If it was a snake it would have bit you," Mother said. That's what you remember, a phrase, an old saying. My sister said, "Grandma told me, 'Never wear horizontal stripes, they make you look fat.' That's one of the few things I remember about Grandma." Or the words disappear and an image remains. I was getting a lecture from my parents about riding my tricycle all the way downtown. I don't remember anything they said. I remember looking out the window, it was just dark, and a block away a man wearing a white shirt and a tie passed under the streetlight and vanished into the night. That's all. Out of a lifetime, a few words, a few pictures, and everything you have lost is lurking there in the dark, poised to strike.

UNCLE AXEL

In the box of old photos there's one of a young man with a moustache wearing a long coat, circa 1890. The photo is labeled "Uncle Karl" on the back. That would be your mother's granduncle, who came from Sweden, a missionary, and was killed by Indians in North Dakota, your great-granduncle. The young man in the photo is looking away from the camera, slightly to the left. He has a look of determination, a man of destiny, preparing to bring the faith to the heathen Sioux. But it isn't Karl. The photo was mislabeled, fifty years ago. It's actually a photo of Uncle Axel, from Norway, your father's uncle, who was a farmer. No one knows that now. No one remembers Axel, or Karl. If you look closely at the photo it almost appears that the young man is speaking, perhaps muttering "I'm Axel damn it. Quit calling me Karl!"

GREAT GRAY OWL

In fact, he does not care who you are. He does know that you are not to be trusted. He fixes you with his yellow-eyed stare, unapologetic, unafraid. This is the extent of the wisdom he has to offer. Any questions you may have you will have to answer for yourself.

III

BALONEY

There's a young couple in the parking lot, kissing. Not just kissing, they look as though they might eat each other up, kissing, nibbling, biting, mouths wide open, play fighting like young dogs, wrapped around each other like snakes. I remember that, sort of, that hunger, that passionate intensity. And I get a kind of nostalgic craving for it, in the way that I get a craving, occasionally, for the food of my childhood. Baloney on white bread, for instance: one slice of white bread with mustard or Miracle Whip or ketchup—not ketchup, one has to draw the line somewhere—and one slice of baloney. It had a nice symmetry to it, the circle of baloney on the rectangle of bread. Then you folded the bread and baloney in the middle and took a bite out of the very center of the folded side. When you unfolded the sandwich you had a hole, a circle in the center of the bread and baloney frame, a window, a porthole from which you could get a new view of the world.

THE BIG BANG

When the morning comes that you don't wake up, what remains of your life goes on as some kind of electromagnetic energy. There's a slight chance you might appear on someone's screen as a dot. Face it. You are a blip or a ping, part of the background noise, the residue of the Big Bang. You remember the Big Bang, don't you? You were about 26 years old, driving a brand new red and white Chevy convertible, with that beautiful blond girl at your side, Charlene, was her name. You had a case of beer on ice in the back, cruising down Highway number 7 on a summer afternoon and then you parked near Loon Lake just as the moon began to rise. Way back then you said to yourself, "Boy, it doesn't get any better than this," and you were right.

PLANTING

I am not planting an acorn from which a mighty and symbolic oak will grow. There is no time for that now. I'll just plant a few seeds, a row of nasturtiums perhaps. I'm not looking for a career. I missed that. I just want a part-time job, nothing too strenuous. Because this isn't about growth or beauty or meaning, it's about the question of whether, at my age, having gotten down in the literal and metaphorical dirt, I can get up again.

FREEZE

Everything in the garden is dead, killed by a sudden hard freeze, the beans, the tomatoes, fruit still clinging to the branches. It's all heaped up ready to go to the compost pile: rhubarb leaves, nasturtiums, pea vines, even the geraniums. It's too bad. The garden was so beautiful, green and fresh, but then we were all beautiful once. Everything dies, we understand. But the mind of the observer, which cannot imagine not imagining, goes on. The dynasties are cut down like the generations of grass, the bodies blacken and turn into coal. The waters rise and cover the earth and the mind broods on the face of the deep, and learns nothing.

MUSHROOM HUNTING

Here I am, as usual, wandering vaguely through a dark wood. Just when I think I know something, when I think I have discerned some pattern, a certain strategy—ah, they grow on the north edge of the low mossy spots— I find one on top of a rise and it shoots my theory all to hell. Every time I find one it's a surprise. The truth is there is no thought that goes into this. These things just pop up. And all this thinking, this human consciousness, isn't what it's cracked up to be. Some inert matter somehow gets itself together, pokes itself up from the ground, gets some ideas and goes walking around, wanting and worrying, gets angry, takes a kick at the dog and falls apart.

THE GREAT PLAINS

I was born around here. It's difficult to pinpoint the exact location because it's all the same, the big empty middle of the country. Over here it's flat as a tabletop, and here it's more rolling. Here's corn, and over there wheat, but don't bother with nuances, really it's all the same. It's cattle and oil. It's "Howdy Jesus! Gimme a Coors." It's wind and dust and tumbleweeds. It's 500 miles before the sun goes down: one little town after another. "How far is it from Cargill to Monsanto Falls?" What do people do here? They live here, same as people live anywhere. They die here too.

Once some friends and I organized a poetry reading tour of regional cemeteries, funded by a grant from the State Arts Board, to pay for the gasoline and the booze. It was an effort to bring some culture to the area. The audiences were not the most responsive. However, I took the fact that there was no coughing or shuffling during my readings as a sign of interest and attentiveness.

THINGS DON'T GO

Things don't go the way you want them to go. If you think the handle turns to the right, it turns to the left. Whichever way you think it turns; it turns the other way. It is no use trying to anticipate this; in every case it goes the other way. There's no use looking for your hat, it's on your head, where you will never see it. Whatever comes to you comes as a gift without your name on it. The moon wanders around the night sky, the sun rises, and a flock of birds lands briefly in the unmown grass.

CROSSROAD BLUES

As these things go, there are no other cars on the road for miles and we arrive simultaneously at the four-way stop at the junction of the Munger-Shaw Road and Yggdrasill Road, he in his big four-by-four Ford pickup and me in my beat-up old Chrysler. Because I'm feeling magnanimous and he's on my right, I motion to him to go ahead. Then he waves me to go first. Then we both start and both come to a sudden halt. I motion again for him to go. Then the son-of-a-bitch flips me the bird. Well, screw you mister, and I flip him the bird right back. Neither of us moves. One of us has to go first but I'll be damned if it's going to be me.

ILLUSION

Is it true that this world, this life, is an illusion, all smoke and mirrors? It must be, because according to a recent poll, seventy percent of the American public believes that Ronald Reagan did a good job as president. And yet if life is only a figment, a feint, a construction of breath and vapor, then why is it a rock falls and smashes your toe and you go hopping around on one foot, mad with pain? Why, if you happen to look at a woman on the sidewalk and your car plows into the truck in front of you, are you dead and no longer allowed to play the game? It's an illusion, but it's a damn good one.

SPIRIT WIND

Car headlights come rushing up from behind, someone doing 80 on this lonely back road, then, just as they get within a hundred yards of the car, the headlights vanish. He couldn't have turned.... And there was the time when something—there was no wind, no one inside the house— slammed the door just as you were about to enter. There is something out there, no doubt, something that defies explanation and that does not necessarily wish you well. But it's best not to go giving it dumb names like "Spirit Wind". Best not say anything about it at all; just keep your big mouth shut. Like that little yellow bird, for instance. I've seen it, tiny yellow bird that flies in and out of your ear. Perhaps it nests there in the top of a tiny banana tree. And when your new lover leans forward for the first time to kiss your delicate shell-like ear, he says, "You've got a banana tree in your ear!" "What?" you say, "I can't hear you...."

MY POEM

I am so pleased that you brought this in. What you have is a masterpiece of its kind: genuine, handcrafted, poetry— I'd say late twentieth century, truly a remarkable work. We here agree that its value, conservatively, is from ten to twelve thousand dollars. But, on a good day with the right buyer it could fetch upwards of fifteen thousand, although the market for this kind of thing is a bit soft right now. Now, you have told me that you will never sell this piece and I think that that is a good idea. However, if I were in the insurance business, I would advise you to insure this fine work for at least thirty thousand dollars. And remember to keep it out of direct sunlight.

COLORS

She said, "I see people as colors. My friend Jenny is yellow or gold." "Because she is blond?" "No it's not that. I think of James, for instance, as black, like a pirate flag, but his hair is quite blond." James was my rival, two years older and in college. "What color are you?" "Oh, I'm spring colors; maybe that bright green that you see when the leaves are still small. Kind of young and dumb." She laughed. She was so beautiful, her hair a wonderful red-gold and her eyes, I thought, green as the spring leaves. I knew I was getting nowhere. "What about me?" I asked. "What color am I?" "Oh, I see you as brown," she said, "shades of brown."

A DISAPPOINTMENT

The best anyone can say about you is that you are a disappointment. We had higher expectations of you. We had hoped that you would finish your schooling. We had hoped that you would have kept your job at the plant. We had hoped that you would have been a better son and a better father. We hoped, and fully expected, that you would finish reading *Moby Dick.* I wish that, when I am talking to you, you would at least raise your head off your desk and look at me. There are people who, without your gifts, have accomplished so much in this life. I am truly disappointed. Your parents, your wife and children, your entire family, in fact, everyone you know is disappointed, deeply disappointed.

A VISIT TO JUNEAU

Juneau is a noisy place in summer, cruise boats arriving and departing, airplanes landing and taking off, seaplanes coming and going, helicopters all in a row—off to look at the glacier. There are fishing boats bringing in their catch, chum salmon doing belly flops in the harbor, automobiles racing around—even though there is really no place you can get to by car. There are people selling jewelry and furs and popcorn and there are tourists everywhere. For a long time this whole area was covered in ice and it was quiet and the big mountains looked silently down on the sea. None of this activity makes any sense, but this is what we do. Apparently, this is our job. So when some guy calls me and wants me to move his refrigerator and paint the floor underneath, it's okay with me.

WISHES

Wishes, if they come true, always have a way of turning out badly. The fisherman's wife got wealth and power but wound up with nothing. Tithonus was given eternal life by Zeus but not eternal youth so the gift had unpleasant consequences. King Midas did not do well with his wish either. Solomon wished for wisdom, got wealth and power besides and still was not a happy man. Suppose you wished to be far away from the stupid, repressive town you grew up in and suddenly you were whirled away in a cloud of dust. Before long some well-intentioned fool would miss you and wish you home again. If you wished for a beautiful woman or a rich and handsome husband you *know* what would happen. What *is* there to wish for finally? A blindfold and a last cigarette? No, we all know how bad smoking is for your health. When the genie comes out of the bottle or the man comes to your door with a check the size of a billboard you should say "No." "No thank you." Say, "I don't want any." Say, "I wish you would go away." But you aren't going to, are you?

WORRY BEADS

For Dennis Matson

The hand is held outward, away from the body in the gesture of one about to shake the hand of another. The string of the worry beads is held between the first and second fingers, at approximately the middle joint of the fingers. The string is attached to a loop of metal beads, which hangs down on the outside of the hand. The loop is flipped up and over the hand with a quick outward motion of the little finger and without turning the wrist. The beads now hang on the inside of the hand. They are now flipped back to their original position with the thumb. Thus to (theoretically) relieve tension and anxiety this action is repeated rapidly many times. After repeated attempts I find I am unable to do this and it worries me.

A CONVERSATION
WITH GARRISON KEILLOR

GK: So what about the brown pills? What are they? We'd all like to know.

LJ: I'm not sure what they are. Someone I trust recommended them. Some kind of oil or essence, but I think they are great. I'd advise you to try them. I'll send some.

GK: Is your friend a veterinarian?

LJ: They are big. I think a horse would have no problem swallowing them. Perhaps they are Marvel Mystery Oil. I think they are really good for you. I think I am much smarter than I used to be. For instance, I don't stay up all night, nowadays, or drive fast, or chase after young women, very often. I take this as a sign of increased intelligence.

GK: When you compare certain people to starfish, in the sense that they have no brain and yet still manage to have a social life, are you referring to specific people? Perhaps some you've met in Minneapolis? Or St. Paul?

LJ: I meet people everywhere who are like that, even in Duluth. I manage an active social life myself.

GK: I know that I've been with you at times when I was dull, so I was checking to make sure that I don't need to take the starfish reference personally. Had I known you were watching so closely, I would've tried harder to be smarter.

LJ: I think that the poet is as much a starfish as anyone else.

GK: Are we to assume that Jane Kieffer of San Diego is a made-up person?

LJ: Jane Kieffer seems like someone I'd like to know.

GK: A real person in San Diego whom you wanted to know?

LJ: Maybe you know Jane Kieffer already.

GK: Is she a famous person who I don't know?

LJ: I've lost touch with JK. I'm sure she was destined for a career.

GK: I love the poem, it's not that. I just want to know more about Jane. Such as how tall she was and why you treated her so badly. Though I'm sure we've all been cruel to lovers in our time. (You were lovers, right?)

LJ: I had my pants off— at least in the poem.

GK: Was she younger than you? Did you let her drive your car? Did you like her hair that way? I just feel there is a whole novel here that is trying to get out.

LJ: It's life. You grab just a bit of it as it goes by and put that bit into a poem, otherwise it would just be made up.

GK: "Just" be made up? Are you sneering at those of us in the fiction profession?

LJ: I'm not trying to belittle fiction writers. I think poets and fiction writers are about the same thing, trying to make sense of our experience. It's just that we have different approaches: condense or expand. I'm a prose poet, who knows where that could lead?

GK: "Afterlife" is a lovely little scene, though one assumes it is "made up". Fiction, in other words, not life, as we know it. Were I to adapt the book into a movie, I'd begin with "Afterlife" And then I'd have you, the poet, in the form of a cloud. You'd be talking and observing things below and looking back ruefully on your life. Or not ruefully, as the case might be. And Jane Kieffer would appear. There would be starfish in the movie and they would eat brown pills and turn into happy dogs. Or I could, for a small additional charge, arrange these prose poems in lines and make them real poems. It wouldn't take me long. I just think it would do something for sales, if you were a poet and not a prose poet.

LJ: Yes, real poets do make a lot more money, movie rights and all that. But I will not be tempted.

Louis Jenkins was born in Oklahoma and is former anchor of the Adams School 220 yard relay team, which was blue ribbon winner in the 1954 all-school Little Olympics. He has worked as, among other jobs, a substitute assistant dough mixer. Since 1970 he has lived in Duluth, Minnesota.